CASH FLOW MASTERY

CASH FL₹W MASTERY

CA Jagmohan Singh

Worldwide Published by
Pendown Press

PENDOWN PRESS LLP
An ISO 9001 & ISO 14001 Certified Co.,
Regd. Office: 3767A, Kanhaiya Nagar,
Tri Nagar, Delhi-110035
Ph.: 8130886000, 9650072927
E-mail: info@pendownpress.com
Branch Office: 1A/2A, 20, Hari Sadan, Ansari Road,
Daryaganj, New Delhi-110002
Ph.: 011-45794768
Website: PendownPress.com

Edition: 2024

ISBN: 978-93-6338-996-0

Layout and Cover Designed by Pendown Graphics Team
Printed and Bound in India by Thomson Press India Ltd.

This book is intended solely for educational purposes. It provides general information to help business owners better understand cash flow management. The author and publisher are not responsible for any financial decisions made based on the information provided herein. Readers are encouraged to consult with a qualified financial advisor for specific guidance.

Dedication

To my mother, ***Harbhajan Kaur,*** *my first* ***'Finance Mentor',*** *whose wisdom and guidance inspired me to help others achieve financial success.*

Table of Contents

Section: 4 - Additional Resources, Inspiration, Tools & Techniques

Acknowledgements

I extend my deepest gratitude to the backbone of the economy—business owners—who tirelessly strive to build, sustain, and grow their enterprises despite challenges. This book, *Cash Flow Mastery*, is a tribute to your dedication, resilience, and unwavering commitment to financial excellence.

To every entrepreneur who has navigated the complexities of cash flow, taken risks, and turned challenges into opportunities, I salute your courage and perseverance. Your stories of struggle and success have been a guiding force in shaping the insights shared in this book.

A special acknowledgment to the business owners who have shared their experiences with me, allowing me to learn from real-world scenarios. Your willingness to open up about your financial challenges has been invaluable in making this book a practical guide for others.

To my clients and participants in my workshops, thank you for your trust and for implementing the strategies discussed here. Your results and feedback continue to inspire my mission of helping businesses achieve financial control and growth.

Lastly, I express my gratitude to my mentors, peers, and the larger business community for their continuous support, insights, and encouragement. Your contributions have helped shape my understanding of cash flow management and enabled me to compile these lessons for the benefit of all entrepreneurs.

This book is for every business owner who aspires to create a cash-rich, financially secure, and thriving enterprise. May your journey toward cash flow mastery be successful and fulfilling.

Thank You!

Bal Raj Goel

❍❍❍❍

Preface

Business owners embark on their entrepreneurial journeys with passion and dreams. However, many find it challenging to sustain and grow due to a lack of effective cash flow management and financial controls. The absence of a robust cash flow system often leads to mismanagement, delayed payments, and even business failures. This book addresses these challenges, offering practical solutions, real-life examples, and global best practices to help entrepreneurs build resilient, cash-rich businesses. Through actionable practices and clear examples from the Indian and global business landscape, this book empowers readers to master their cash flow and ensure long-term success.

About The Author
CA Jagmohan Singh

CA Jagmohan Singh is a renowned **Cash Flow** Coach with over 25 years of experience in Cash Flow management and business consulting. Over the years, he has worked with businesses ranging from small startups to large established enterprises across **India, USA** and **Canada**. His ability to transform cash flow strategies into actionable insights has led to significant growth for many businesses. Jagmohan Singh has delivered keynote speeches at numerous conferences and summits, sharing his expertise on cash flow management. He is also an advocate for financial literacy among SMEs and believes in empowering entrepreneurs with the tools and knowledge to thrive in competitive markets.

He is famous for his 5am Cash Flow Mastery Videos, which are published every saturday on YouTube Channel "Jagmohan Singh Cash Flow Coach"

He is a rank holder Chartered Accountant. He has been awarded as Global Indian of the year 2022 at London, thereafter awarded as Best Cash Flow Coach in the year 2023 by Times of India Group and Asia's greatest leader in Cash Flow award by Asia One Magazine in the year 2024.

He is the author of #1 bestseller book on amazon in the name of Financial Freedom with Financial Control.

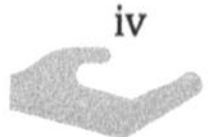

About the Book: Cash Flow Mastery by CA Jagmohan Singh

Introduction

Cash *Flow Mastery* is an essential guide for business owners and entrepreneurs who want to master financial stability and business growth by effectively managing their cash flow. Written by CA Jagmohan Singh, a seasoned Cash Flow Coach, this book provides practical insights, real-life case studies, and actionable strategies to help businesses thrive.

Objective of the Book

The book aims to:

- Educate business owners on the importance of cash flow management.
- Bust common myths and misconceptions about cash flow.
- Provide solutions to common financial problems faced by businesses.
- Offer global best practices, tools, and techniques for effective cash flow management.
- Empower entrepreneurs with actionable steps to build a cash-rich business.

Structure of the Book

The book is divided into four key sections:

1. **Understanding Cash Flow**
    - Why cash flow is crucial for business success.
    - Common myths and misunderstandings about cash flow.

- Real-world examples of businesses facing cash flow misinterpretation.
- Strategies to build a cash flow-positive business.

2. **Problems in Cash Flow and Their Solutions**
    - Identifying common cash flow challenges like poor receivables management, high fixed costs, inventory mismanagement, and more.
    - Case studies demonstrating how businesses successfully overcame these issues.
    - Step-by-step solutions to improve cash flow.
3. **The Way Forward: Navigating the Future**
    - The choice between self-managing cash flow or seeking expert guidance.
    - A structured approach to mastering cash flow with expert support.
    - The role of financial forecasting in ensuring business sustainability.
4. **Additional Resources, Tools, and Techniques**
    - Indian and global case studies on cash flow success.
    - Best financial tools and software for managing cash flow.
    - Techniques for financial contingency planning.
    - Inspirational stories from business leaders who mastered cash flow.

Key Takeaways

Cash Flow is More Important Than Profit: Even profitable businesses can fail due to poor cash flow management.

- **Automation and Technology:** Utilizing digital tools like Zoho Books, QuickBooks, and Tally can streamline cash flow tracking.
- **Proactive Planning:** Forecasting cash flow and planning for contingencies can prevent financial crises.
- **Global Best Practices:** Learning from international business strategies can help Indian businesses improve financial resilience.

Who Should Read This Book?

This book is ideal for:

- Business owners and entrepreneurs.
- Startups and SMEs struggling with financial planning.
- Financial professionals and consultants.
- Anyone looking to gain a deep understanding of business cash flow.

SECTION 1

UNDERSTANDING CASH FLOW

CHAPTER 1

Why Cash Flow is so Important

The Turnaround Story of Sachin: Mastering Cash Flow to Revive a Business

---

Sachin was a dedicated businessman running a mid-sized manufacturing unit in Mumbai. His business produced high-quality custom packaging solutions, which had earned him a loyal clientele and a reputation for innovation. Despite this, Sachin faced a persistent challenge: cash flow issues.

His company generated significant revenue, but the cash seemed to vanish as quickly as it came in. Payments to suppliers were often delayed, creating bottlenecks in production. These delays led to missed delivery deadlines, frustrated clients, and a declining reputation in the market. The pressure mounted, and Sachin began to question whether his business could survive.

One evening, Sachin decided to confront the issue head-on. He reached out to a cash flow coach, who helped him identify the root causes of his financial struggles. Together, they devised a structured plan to transform the way his business managed cash flow.

The Action Plan

1. **Automating Invoicing Systems:** Sachin implemented an automated invoicing system, ensuring that invoices were

generated and sent out as soon as goods were delivered. The system included reminders for overdue payments, reducing the time and effort his team spent chasing clients for money. This step streamlined cash inflow and improved the visibility of outstanding receivables.

2. **Negotiating Better Payment Terms with Vendors:** Sachin approached his key suppliers with a clear plan. He shared his vision for stabilizing the business and requested extended payment terms. By building trust and showing commitment to timely payments, he successfully negotiated 60-day payment cycles instead of the previous 30 days. This gave him breathing room to align outgoing payments with incoming cash.
3. **Implementing Stricter Credit Control Policies:** Recognizing that leniency in offering credit was a major issue, Sachin introduced stricter credit control measures. New clients were required to provide partial upfront payments, and existing clients with a history of delayed payments were put on shorter credit terms. His team also conducted regular creditworthiness assessments.

The Results

The changes began to show results within just a few months. With automated invoicing, payments from clients became more predictable. The extended terms with suppliers allowed Sachin to prioritize timely procurement of raw materials, ensuring smooth production. Stricter credit policies reduced the risk of bad debts and improved cash flow reliability.

By the end of six months, Sachin's business had not only stabilized but also flourished. The newfound efficiency led to a

30% increase in profit margins. Delays were a thing of the past, and his improved reliability helped him regain the trust of both suppliers and clients. For the first time in years, Sachin could see a clear path to scaling his business further.

Lessons Learned

Sachin's story serves as a powerful reminder for business owners that revenue alone does not guarantee success. Managing cash flow effectively is critical to sustaining and growing a business. By focusing on processes and building trust with stakeholders, Sachin turned a struggling enterprise into a thriving venture, proving that the right strategies can unlock any business's true potential.

❍❍❍❍

CHAPTER 2

Seven Myths in Cash Flow and the Reality

Cash flow is the lifeblood of any business, yet it is often misunderstood due to common myths and misconceptions.

Here are seven myths about cash flow and the corresponding realities that every business owner should know.

Myth 1: Profit Equals Cash Flow

Reality

Profit and cash flow are not the same. Profit is the financial gain after subtracting expenses from revenue, but it does not account for the timing of cash inflows and outflows. A business can be profitable on paper but still face cash flow challenges if receivables are delayed or expenses are mismanaged.

Example

A company might report a profit of ₹10 lakh in a quarter but struggle to pay suppliers because most of the revenue is tied up in unpaid invoices.

Myth 2: Cash Flow Problems Occur Only in Struggling Businesses

Reality

Even successful businesses with strong sales can experience cash flow issues. Growth often requires significant upfront investments in inventory, staff, or equipment, which can outpace incoming cash. Misalignment between revenue growth and cash flow management can lead to a liquidity crunch.

Example

A fast-growing e-commerce business may face cash shortages while waiting for customer payments during peak seasons.

Myth 3: More Sales Automatically Improve Cash Flow

Reality

While sales are important, they do not guarantee improved cash flow. Increased sales often bring higher costs in the form of raw materials, production, logistics, or credit offered to customers. Without proper controls, growing sales can worsen cash flow issues.

Example

A company offering extended credit to boost sales might find itself with high receivables but no liquidity to pay immediate expenses.

Myth 4: Cash Flow Management is Only About Cutting Costs

Reality

Effective cash flow management involves a combination of strategies, not just cost-cutting. It includes optimizing receivables, managing payables, maintaining healthy reserves, and ensuring efficient capital allocation. Cost-cutting alone cannot solve deeper structural issues.

Example

A business might negotiate better terms with suppliers or accelerate customer payments rather than just reducing marketing expenses.

Myth 5: Borrowing Always Solves Cash Flow Problems

Reality

While borrowing can provide temporary relief, it is not a sustainable solution to cash flow issues. Loans and credit come with interest and repayment obligations, which can worsen financial strain if the root causes of cash flow problems are not addressed.

Example

A business relying on loans to cover operating expenses might accumulate debt, leading to financial instability in the long term.

Myth 6: Cash Flow is Only About Inflows

Reality

Cash flow is about both inflows and outflows. Businesses must track and manage not just incoming payments but also expenses such as salaries, rent, utilities, and loan repayments. Ignoring outflows can lead to liquidity crises even with strong inflows.

Example

A manufacturing firm with irregular cash outflow tracking might face a sudden inability to pay vendors, disrupting production.

Myth 7: Cash Flow is a One-Time Fix

Reality

Cash flow management is an ongoing process. Business dynamics, market conditions, and customer behaviors evolve, requiring constant monitoring and adjustments. A one-time strategy cannot ensure sustainable cash flow health.

Example:

An exporter's cash flow might stabilize after implementing payment terms for one client but require adjustments when dealing with another client in a different country with varying credit policies.

The Way Forward: Cash Flow Realities

Understanding these myths and realities empowers businesses to take proactive measures for cash flow management. Key strategies include:

1. **Automation:** Use tools for invoicing and tracking cash flow to avoid delays.

2. **Negotiation:** Work with vendors and clients to establish favorable terms.
3. **Monitoring:** Regularly review cash flow statements and forecasts to anticipate challenges.
4. **Credit Control:** Implement policies to minimize receivable delays and bad debts.
5. **Diversification:** Balance customer and supplier portfolios to reduce dependency on a few accounts.

By addressing these myths and embracing the realities, businesses can ensure a steady cash flow, build resilience, and achieve long-term success.

CHAPTER 3

Examples of Cash Flow Misinterpretation

It is important to clearly understand what cash flow is, very often business owners create crises for themselves by misinterpreting other things as cash flow as illustrated by the examples below—-

Example 1: Revenue vs. Receivables

A retail chain in Delhi misinterpreted its revenue figures as cash inflow. By ignoring receivable timelines, they faced a liquidity crunch during peak season, and, as a result, they were unable to restock inventory.

The Lesson: Always distinguish between revenue earned and cash in hand.

Example 2: Expense Allocation

A tech startup in Bengaluru treated capital expenses as operational costs, creating a skewed cash flow statement. This mistake led to underestimating the required working capital.

The Lesson: Businesses must categorize expenses accurately to maintain clarity.

❍❍❍❍

CHAPTER 4

The Real Solution to Managing Cash Flow

Effectively managing cash flow is not just about addressing isolated financial issues; it requires a holistic approach encompassing daily monitoring, strategic planning, and proactive measures. Here's a detailed exploration of a comprehensive cash flow management system:

1. Daily Tracking

Why It's Important:

Daily tracking provides real-time insights into your financial health. Knowing exactly where your money is going and coming from helps you avoid surprises and ensures better decision-making.

How to Implement:

- **Use Tools:** Implement software like Tally, Zoho Books, or QuickBooks for real-time tracking of inflows and outflows.
- **Set Alerts:** Automate reminders for due payments and pending receivables to avoid missed deadlines.
- **Segregate Expenses:** Categorize expenses into fixed, variable, and discretionary. This allows you to prioritize payments and defer non-essential spending if needed.

Example:

A manufacturing unit tracks daily collections and notices a pattern of delayed payments from a key client. With this insight, they adjust their credit terms to align better with cash flow needs.

2. Reserve Building

Why It's Important:

Unforeseen expenses or emergencies—like a sudden machinery breakdown or a client delaying payments—can severely impact cash flow. Building a reserve acts as a safety net during such instances.

How to Implement:

- **Allocate a Percentage:** Dedicate at least 10% of your monthly revenues to a contingency fund.
- **Separate Account:** Keep the reserve in a separate bank account to prevent accidental use.
- **Automate Savings:** Use auto-transfer options to move funds into the reserve account monthly.

Example:

An IT services firm saves ₹50,000 monthly in a contingency fund. When a major client delays payment for three months, the company uses the reserve to cover salaries without borrowing.

3. Vendor Negotiations

Why It's Important:

Vendors are a critical part of the supply chain. Extending payment terms can free up cash for immediate operational needs, while early payment incentives help foster goodwill and maintain supply stability.

How to Implement:

- **Understand Vendor Needs:** Approach vendors with a collaborative mindset. Highlight mutual benefits and establish trust.
- **Negotiate Terms:** Aim for longer payment cycles (e.g., 60-90 days) without affecting supply quality.
- **Leverage Discounts:** If you have surplus cash, use it to pay early and gain discounts.

Example:

A retailer negotiates 90-day payment terms with its supplier but offers a 2% early payment for invoices settled within 30 days. This flexibility helps the retailer manage cash more efficiently.

4. Customer Policies

Why It's Important:

Delayed receivables are a primary cause of cash flow issues. Encouraging prompt payments improves liquidity and ensures a steady cash inflow.

How to Implement:

- **Offer Early Payment Discounts:** Provide a discount of 1-2% for customers who settle invoices within 7-10 days.
- **Charge Penalties:** Enforce penalties for late payments to discourage delays.
- **Invoice Promptly:** Automate invoice generation and delivery to minimize delays in receivables.

Example:

A B2B company offering a 2% discount for early payments sees a significant improvement in cash inflows as 60% of its clients take advantage of the incentive.

5. Forecasting Cash Flow

Why It's Important:

Forecasting helps anticipate cash shortages and surpluses, enabling proactive measures rather than reactive fixes.

How to Implement:

- **Create Projections:** Use historical data to forecast cash flow for the next 3, 6, and 12 months.
- **Scenario Planning:** Develop best-case, worst-case, and realistic scenarios to prepare for uncertainties.
- **Integrate Departments:** Align sales, procurement, and operations teams to ensure accuracy in forecasts.

Example:

An event management company forecasts a cash shortage during the off-season and proactively arranges a short-term line of credit.

6. Managing Inventory Levels

Why It's Important:

Excess inventory ties up cash, while insufficient inventory can disrupt operations. Striking a balance ensures smoother cash flow.

How to Implement:

- **Optimize Stock Levels:** Use inventory management tools to track and reorder stock as needed.
- **Just-in-Time (JIT) Model:** Adopt a JIT approach to minimize holding costs.
- **Liquidate Slow-Moving Stock:** Offer discounts to clear slow-moving inventory and free up cash.

Example:

A wholesaler identifies excess stock through tracking software and runs a clearance sale, unlocking ₹5 lakh in cash.

7. Diversify Income Streams

Why It's Important:

Relying on a few customers or income streams increases cash flow risk. Diversification provides stability and minimizes dependence.

How to Implement:

- **Add Revenue Channels:** Explore complementary products or services.
- **Expand Customer Base:** Target new markets or industries to reduce reliance on a few clients.
- **Focus on Retainers:** Secure long-term contracts with predictable payment terms.

Example:

A digital marketing agency adds website development services, creating a new revenue stream that offsets fluctuations in ad campaign income.

The Comprehensive System in Action

Adopting this cash flow management system ensures not just stability but also growth:

1. Daily tracking prevents missed opportunities or unnoticed leaks.
2. Reserve building provides confidence to navigate uncertainties.

3. Vendor negotiations create flexibility in outflows.
4. Customer policies accelerate inflows.
5. Forecasting prepares you for future needs and prevents surprises.
6. Inventory management optimizes working capital.

Diversification reduces risks and promotes long-term success.

When combined, these strategies create a robust framework for sustained cash flow management, ensuring businesses remain resilient and profitable in any market condition.

❍❍❍❍

SECTION 2

PROBLEMS IN CASH FLOW AND THEIR SOLUTIONS

This Section Focuses on the Comprehensive Analysis of Cash Flow Problems and Solutions

Cash flow problems can severely hinder business operations and growth. Here's an in-depth exploration of seven common cash flow problems, the history behind them, the typical wrong actions taken, the best solutions, and detailed case studies to illustrate the practical application of these solutions.

CHAPTER 5

Problem 1: Poor Receivables Management

Definition:

Poor receivables management refers to delayed payments from customers, resulting in a lack of liquid cash to meet operational expenses.

History Around the Problem:

As businesses expanded, the practice of offering credit to customers became standard, especially in B2B environments. However, this also led to delayed payments, often due to inefficiencies in invoicing, follow-ups, or weak credit control policies.

Mistakes Business Owners Make:

- Offering unlimited credit without assessing customer reliability.
- Ignoring overdue payments to maintain customer relationships.
- Relying on manual invoicing, leading to errors and delays.
- Writing off bad debts as inevitable.

The Best Solution:

- **Automate Invoicing:** Implement software that sends invoices immediately upon delivery and tracks payment statuses.

- **Set Clear Terms:** Define payment terms (e.g., 30 days) upfront and communicate them clearly.
- **Follow Up Regularly:** Use automated reminders and personal follow-ups to ensure timely payments.
- **Offer Incentives and Penalties:** Encourage early payments with discounts and discourage delays with penalties.

Freed Up Rs. 30 Lakhs in Just Months

A Case Study

The Client: A textile business in Surat.

The Issue: They faced receivable delays averaging 90 days, causing cash shortages.

Suggested Solution: The owner was advised to implement automated invoicing using Zoho Books, set payment reminders, and introduce a 2% penalty for delays beyond 30 days.

The Results: Within six months—

- The receivable period dropped to 45 days.
- The business freed up Rs.30 lakhs.
- This sum was reinvested into purchasing raw materials.
- This boosted production by 20%.

❍❍❍❍

CHAPTER 6

Problem 2: High Fixed Costs

Definition:

Fixed costs like rent, utilities, and salaries remain constant regardless of revenue fluctuations, straining cash flow during slow periods.

History Around the Problem:

Fixed costs became prominent during the Industrial Revolution as businesses invested in infrastructure and labor. However, a lack of adaptability to modern cost-saving measures has led to inefficiencies.

Mistakes Business Owners Make

- Over-investing in office spaces or equipment without considering scalability.
- Maintaining excessive in-house staff instead of outsourcing.
- Avoiding regular audits of fixed costs.

The Best Solution:

- **Review Expenses:** Conduct periodic audits to identify and eliminate unnecessary costs.
- **Outsource Non-Core Activities:** Shift functions like logistics, IT, or HR to third-party providers to reduce fixed costs.
- **Negotiate Contracts:** Renegotiate rents and utility rates to align with market conditions.

Reduced Cost & Increased Production Efficiency by 25%

A Case Study

The Client: A manufacturing unit in Pune.

The Issue: Incurring high logistics costs.

Suggested Solution: To outsource their delivery operations to a third-party logistics provider.

The Results—--

- This reduced fixed costs by 15%, saving ₹1.2 crores annually.
- The savings were used to upgrade machinery.
- This increased production efficiency by 25%

CHAPTER 7

Problem 3: Inventory Mismanagement

Definition:

Holding excess or insufficient inventory leads to cash being tied up in stock or lost sales due to unavailability.

History Around the Problem:

Traditional inventory practices focused on stockpiling to avoid shortages, but this led to high holding costs and wastage.

Mistakes Business Owners Make:

- Overstocking to avoid potential shortages.
- Failing to track inventory turnover and expiry.
- Neglecting demand forecasting.

The Best Solution:

- **Implement JIT Systems:** Reduce inventory levels by aligning purchases with demand.
- **Conduct Regular Audits:** Identify and liquidate slow-moving or obsolete stock.
- **Use Inventory Software:** Automate tracking and forecasting for better stock management.

Reduced Wastage by 20% & Increased Sales by 15%

A Case Study

The Client: A pharmaceutical company in Hyderabad.

The Issue: Unnecessary Inventory Wastage.

Suggested Solution: To conduct monthly inventory audits and adopt JIT principles.

The Result—-

- This reduced wastage by 20%, saving ₹50 lakhs annually.
- The freed up cash was used to expand their distribution network, increasing sales by 15%.

❍❍❍❍

CHAPTER 8

Problem 4: Lack of Financial Forecasting

Definition:

Inadequate forecasting leads to unpreparedness for future cash requirements, resulting in operational disruptions.

History Around the Problem

Historically, small businesses often relied on gut feelings rather than structured forecasting. As markets became complex, this approach proved insufficient.

Mistakes Business Owners Make:

- Ignoring seasonal trends and upcoming obligations.
- Failing to use forecasting tools.
- Reacting to cash shortages instead of planning proactively.

The Best Solution

- **Adopt Forecasting Tools:** Use software like Tally or QuickBooks to predict cash flow needs.
- **Analyze Historical Data:** Identify patterns in sales and expenses.
- **Scenario Planning:** Prepare for best-case, worst-case, and realistic scenarios.

Using Forecasting Tools Effectively

A Case Study

The Client: A retail chain in Bengaluru.

Implementation: The company used forecasting tools to anticipate a seasonal sales dip during monsoons. The business arranged short-term credit beforehand, ensuring uninterrupted operations.

The Result: As a result, it avoided penalties for delayed supplier payments and maintained customer satisfaction.

❍❍❍❍

CHAPTER 9

Problem 5: Inconsistent Payment Cycles

Definition:

Irregular payment cycles from clients lead to mismatches in cash inflows and outflows, creating liquidity gaps.

History Around the Problem:

With the rise of credit sales, inconsistent payment cycles became a common challenge, especially for businesses dependent on large clients.

Mistakes Business Owners Make:

- Overlooking client payment behavior.
- Accepting client terms without negotiation.
- Offering credit indiscriminately.

The Best Solution:

- **Set Standard Terms:** Establish uniform payment cycles (e.g., 30 days) across clients.
- **Enforce Penalties:** Charge late fees for overdue payments.
- **Diversify Client Base:** Reduce reliance on clients with erratic payment histories.

Reduced Delayed Payments by 40%

A Case Study

The Client: A consultancy firm in Delhi.

The Issue: Delayed payments.

Suggested Solution: Standardizing payment terms and implementing a 2% late payment penalty.

The Result—-

- This reduced delayed payments by 40%.
- This stabilized monthly cash inflows, allowing the business to invest in employee training.

CHAPTER 10

Problem 6: Overdependence on Credit

Definition:

Excessive reliance on borrowed funds increases financial strain due to interest and repayment obligations.

History Around the Problem:

Post-globalization, easy access to credit led businesses to borrow excessively without sustainable repayment strategies.

Mistakes Business Owners Make:

- Using loans for day-to-day operations.
- Ignoring high-interest rates.
- Neglecting reserve building.

The Best Solution:

- **Limit Borrowing:** Reserve credit for critical investments.
- **Build a Cash Reserve:** Allocate a portion of revenue for operational needs.
- **Optimize Cash Flow:** Improve receivables and payables management.

Saved 5 Lakh & Launched a New Product Line

A Case Study

The Client: An SME in Chennai.

The Implementation: Reduced its loan dependency by allocating 10% of revenue to a reserve fund.

The Result—

- Over a year, the company saved ₹5 lakhs in interest payments.
- This was used to launch a new product line.

❍❍❍❍

CHAPTER 11

Problem 7: Ignoring Contingency Planning

Definition:

Failing to prepare for emergencies can lead to severe cash shortages during unforeseen events.

History Around the Problem:

Many businesses, particularly SMEs, underestimated risks until the COVID-19 pandemic exposed vulnerabilities.

Mistakes Business Owners Make:

- Operating without an emergency fund.
- Overlooking insurance for critical assets.
- Reacting instead of preparing for risks.

The Best Solution:

- **Emergency Fund:** Set aside 5-10% of revenue for unforeseen events.
- **Invest in Insurance:** Protect key assets and operations.
- **Develop Crisis Protocols:** Plan for potential disruptions.

Sustained Production & Client Trust

A Case Study

The Client: A food processing company in Ahmedabad.

The Issue: They faced a sudden raw material shortage due to a strike.

The Solution: Their contingency fund covered alternate sourcing costs.

The Result—

- The decision prevented production halts and maintained client trust.

❍❍❍❍

SECTION 3

THE WAY FORWARD-
NAVIGATING THE FUTURE

CHAPTER 12

Two Choices for Mastering Cash Flow

Do It Yourself or Take Expert Support

In your journey to mastering cash flow management, you have two paths to choose from:

1. **Do It Yourself (DIY)** - Implement cash flow strategies on your own.
2. **Take Support from a Cash Flow Expert -** Collaborate with a professional like CA Jagmohan Singh, who can guide you with expertise and proven frameworks.

This chapter outlines these two choices in detail, helping you decide which approach aligns best with your goals, resources, and business needs. A self-assessment checklist is included to guide your decision.

Choice 1: Do It Yourself (DIY)

If you're confident in your ability to implement cash flow strategies, the DIY route allows you to take control and learn through hands-on experience. This option is suitable for business owners who:

- ➢ Have a foundational understanding of financial management.
- ➢ Are willing to invest time in learning and implementation.
- ➢ Prefer cost-saving options over professional consultation.

What DIY Involves:

1. **Learning Cash Flow Fundamentals:**
   - Understand concepts like inflows, outflows, working capital, and cash reserves.
   - Study tools like cash flow statements and forecasting models.
2. **Using Technology:**
   - Invest in software like Tally, Zoho Books, or QuickBooks to automate invoicing, track expenses, and forecast cash flows.
3. **Implementing Strategies:**
   - Optimize receivables by automating reminders and offering early payment discounts.
   - Negotiate better terms with vendors.
   - Regularly review expenses and identify cost-saving opportunities.
4. **Continuous Monitoring:**
   - Track cash flow daily and adjust strategies based on performance.

Benefits of DIY:

- **Cost-Effective:** No need to pay professional fees.
- **Learning Opportunity:** Gain in-depth financial knowledge.
- **Control:** Make decisions independently without external input.

Challenges of DIY:

- **Time-Intensive:** Requires dedicated time for learning and execution.

- **Risk of Mistakes:** Limited expertise may lead to errors.
- **Overwhelm:** Managing multiple financial aspects can be stressful.

Choice 2: Take Support from a Cash Flow Expert

Collaborating with a cash flow expert like CA Jagmohan Singh ensures that your business receives personalized, professional guidance.

This option is ideal for business owners who:

- ➢ Struggle with persistent cash flow challenges.
- ➢ Lack the time or expertise to manage finances independently.
- ➢ Want faster results with minimal trial and error.

What Expert Support Involves:

1. **Comprehensive Cash Flow Assessment:**
    - Analyze your current cash flow, identify pain points, and uncover hidden opportunities.
2. **Customized Strategies:**
    - Develop tailored plans to optimize receivables, control expenses, and build reserves.
    - Implement advanced tools and processes for seamless cash flow management.
3. **Ongoing Monitoring and Guidance:**
    - Regular reviews of cash flow performance.
    - Adjust strategies based on market changes and business needs.
4. **Access to Expertise and Resources:**
    - Benefit from proven frameworks and insights.
    - Avoid costly mistakes with expert advice.

Benefits of Expert Support:

- **Time-Saving:** Focus on core business activities while an expert handles cash flow.
- **Minimized Risk:** Rely on professional expertise for accurate and effective solutions.
- **Accelerated Growth:** Achieve results faster through structured implementation.

Challenges of Expert Support:

- **Cost:** Involves professional fees.
- **Dependency:** Some business owners may feel less in control (however, that's only an illusion and mindset).

Self-Assessment Checklist: Should You DIY or Seek Expert Support?

Answer the following questions honestly to determine the best choice for you:

Question	Yes	No
Do you understand financial statements and cash flow?		
Are you comfortable using accounting and cash flow tools?		
Can you dedicate time to learning and implementing strategies?		
Have you successfully managed cash flow challenges in the past?		
Do you have a clear roadmap for improving cash flow?		

Scoring Guide:

- **Mostly Yes:** You are well-suited for the DIY approach.
- **Mostly No:** Consider seeking professional support to avoid costly mistakes and achieve faster results.

Why Choose CA Jagmohan Singh as Your Cash Flow Expert?

CA Jagmohan Singh is a seasoned professional with years of experience helping businesses transform their cash flow management. Here's what you gain by collaborating with him:

- **Proven Expertise:** Access, tested frameworks that deliver results.
- **Personalized Attention:** Receive customized solutions tailored to your unique business needs.
- **Educational Guidance:** Learn cash flow principles alongside expert implementation.
- **Confidence and Peace of Mind:** Focus on growing your business while leaving cash flow management to an expert.

Next Steps: Taking Action

1 **DIY:**
   - Download free resources like cash flow templates and guides from JSAOnline.in.
   - Attend a free webinar hosted by CA Jagmohan Singh to learn cash flow basics.

2. **Expert Support:**
   - Schedule a consultation with CA Jagmohan Singh.
   - Enroll in the **Cash Flow Retainership Program** for ongoing guidance and support.

By choosing the right path—whether DIY or expert support—you can take charge of your cash flow and unlock your business's full potential. Remember, the choice is yours, and both paths can lead to success when approached with commitment and determination.

SECTION 4

ADDITIONAL RESOURCES, INSPIRATION, TOOLS & TECHNIQUES

CHAPTER 13

Indian Case Studies

Success Stories of Businesses that Mastered Cash Flow

Mastering cash flow is not just about managing finances; it's about empowering businesses to thrive in challenging environments. These real-life success stories from various industries in India highlight how businesses overcame cash flow hurdles and achieved remarkable growth. Let these stories inspire you to take charge of your financial health.

1. Textile Exporter in Surat: Unlocking ₹50 Lakh in Working Capital

---

The Challenge:

The textile exporter in Surat faced prolonged receivable periods of up to 90 days, leading to cash shortages. Delayed payments from international buyers disrupted their ability to purchase raw materials, affecting production timelines and client satisfaction.

The Strategy:

- **Automated Invoicing:** Implemented Zoho Books for automated invoice generation and tracking.
- **Payment Reminders:** Sent regular reminders to clients about upcoming and overdue payments.

- **Incentives and Penalties:** Introduced a 2% discount for payments made within 15 days and a 1.5% penalty for delays beyond 30 days.

The Result:

The receivable period dropped from 90 days to 45 days. This unlocked ₹50 lakh in working capital, which was reinvested into procuring raw materials in bulk at discounted rates. The business improved production capacity by 30% and established stronger relationships with suppliers and clients.

Key Takeaway:

Streamlined receivables management can significantly improve liquidity and operational efficiency, even in export-dependent industries.

2. Restaurant Chain in Bengaluru: Reducing Pilferage by 20%

The Challenge:

A popular restaurant chain in Bengaluru struggled with cash pilferage and discrepancies in daily sales reporting. This led to frequent cash shortages, making it difficult to manage day-to-day expenses.

The Strategy:

- **Daily Cash Reconciliation:** Introduced a system for reconciling cash at the end of each shift.
- **POS Integration:** Upgraded to a Point-of-Sale (POS) system that tracked every transaction in real-time.
- **Staff Training:** Conducted workshops for staff to emphasize accountability and transparency.

The Result:

The restaurant reduced cash pilferage by 20%, saving ₹12 lakhs annually. These savings were used to open a new outlet, expanding the chain's footprint and increasing overall revenue by 15%.

Key Takeaway:

Implementing daily cash reconciliation and technology integration ensures greater control over cash flow in retail and hospitality businesses.

3. E-Commerce Startup in Noida: Bridging Cash Flow Gaps with Analytics

The Challenge:

An e-commerce startup in Noida experienced cash flow gaps due to inconsistent customer payment cycles and high marketing expenses. This made it challenging to sustain growth and manage inventory during peak seasons.

The Strategy:

- **Data Analytics:** Used advanced analytics tools to forecast cash flow gaps based on historical sales and payment trends.
- **Secured Funding:** Partnered with a fintech lender to secure short-term funding before anticipated gaps.
- **Dynamic Expense Management:** Adjusted marketing spend based on real-time cash flow data.

The Result:

The startup bridged its cash flow gaps during the festive season, ensuring inventory availability and on-time deliveries. Sales grew by 25%, and timely funding helped them avoid penalties and maintain supplier trust.

Key Takeaway:

Leveraging data analytics and securing timely funding can help startups navigate cash flow challenges and scale rapidly.

4. Pharmaceutical Company in Hyderabad: Cutting Wastage by 20%

The Challenge:

A pharmaceutical company in Hyderabad faced high wastage due to overstocking and expired inventory. This led to substantial cash being locked in unusable stock, affecting their working capital.

The Strategy:

- **Inventory Audits:** Conducted monthly audits to identify slow-moving and obsolete inventory.
- **Just-in-Time System:** Adopted a Just-in-Time (JIT) approach to synchronize inventory purchases with demand.
- **Demand Forecasting:** Improved forecasting by analyzing historical sales data and seasonal trends.

The Result:

Wastage was reduced by 20%, freeing up ₹35 lakhs annually. This cash was reinvested into R&D, allowing the company to launch a new product line, increasing market share by 10%.

Key Takeaway:

Regular inventory audits and efficient stock management can significantly reduce waste and free up cash for growth initiatives.

5. Agri-Business in Punjab: Managing Seasonal Income Cycles

The Challenge:

An agri-business in Punjab experienced extreme cash flow fluctuations due to seasonal income cycles. During off-seasons, they struggled to cover operational expenses and repay loans.

The Strategy:

- **Seasonal Forecasting:** Created detailed cash flow forecasts for peak and off-seasons.
- **Reserve Building:** Allocated 10% of peak-season profits to an emergency fund.
- **Flexible Loan Repayments:** Negotiated seasonal repayment terms with banks to align with their income cycle.

The Result:

The business achieved financial stability throughout the year, even during lean periods. The reserve fund and seasonal loan repayments enabled them to invest in mechanized farming equipment, increasing productivity by 40%.

Key Takeaway:

Seasonal businesses can thrive by aligning cash flow strategies with income cycles and building reserves for lean periods.

Lessons Learned from These Success Stories

- **Adapt Technology:** Use tools like POS systems, data analytics, and automation to enhance cash flow management.
- **Be Proactive:** Anticipate challenges through forecasting and audits rather than reacting to crises.
- **Communicate and Negotiate:** Build stronger relationships with customers, suppliers, and lenders through clear communication and favorable terms.
- **Invest Savings Wisely:** Reinvest cash flow improvements into growth areas like R&D, marketing, or expansion.

Your Next Step

These stories prove that with the right strategies, tools, and mindset, any business can overcome cash flow challenges and achieve sustainable growth. Whether you're managing receivables, reducing waste, or preparing for seasonal cycles, mastering cash flow is key to unlocking your business's full potential.

If you're ready to take charge of your cash flow journey, explore **DIY resources** or connect with **CA Jagmohan Singh** for personalized support. The success stories above could soon include yours!

CHAPTER 14

Global Cash Flow Practices and Tools

Managing cash flow effectively is a universal challenge that businesses worldwide face. However, the approaches and tools adopted by different regions vary, reflecting unique business environments and cultures. This chapter delves into global cash flow practices, advanced tools, and insights to help businesses stay competitive and resilient.

Popular Tools for Cash Flow Management

1. QuickBooks

- **What It Does:** QuickBooks is an intuitive accounting software widely used by small and medium-sized businesses (SMBs). It offers features for managing cash flow, invoicing, payroll, and reporting.
- **Key Features:**
  - Automated invoicing and payment reminders.
  - Cash flow projections based on historical data.
  - Integration with bank accounts for real-time tracking of inflows and outflows.
  - Easy-to-read cash flow statements and dashboards.

- **Best For:** SMBs looking for an affordable, user-friendly tool to manage their finances.

2. Zoho Books

- **What It Does:** Zoho Books is an online accounting software that streamlines cash flow management for businesses of all sizes. Its cloud-based nature allows users to access their accounts from anywhere.
- **Key Features:**
  - Invoice automation with multi-currency support.
  - Cash flow forecasting and tracking in real-time.
  - Expense categorization and approvals.
  - Integration with other Zoho apps and third-party tools.
- **Best For:** Businesses seeking a scalable solution with robust automation features.

3. SAP

- **What It Does:** SAP is an enterprise-grade software that provides comprehensive financial management capabilities, including cash flow optimization.
- Key Features:
  - Advanced cash flow forecasting and liquidity management.
  - Multi-location and multi-entity financial consolidation.
  - Integration with supply chain and inventory systems for seamless data flow.
  - AI-powered insights for predictive cash flow analysis.

- **Best For:** Large organizations requiring detailed cash flow management across global operations.

4. Microsoft Excel (Advanced Templates)

- **What It Does:** Microsoft Excel remains a versatile tool for businesses, offering the flexibility to create custom cash flow management systems using advanced formulas and templates.
- **Key Features:**
  - Tailored cash flow templates to track inflows and outflows.
  - Advanced functions like pivot tables, VLOOKUP, and conditional formatting for detailed analysis.
  - Macros for automating repetitive tasks.
  - Visual dashboards for easy interpretation of financial data.
- **Best For:** Businesses with unique needs that prefer customizable and low-cost solutions.

Global Insights: Best Practices from Around the World

---

1. American Businesses: Emphasis on Digital Invoicing

- **Practice:** U.S. businesses focus heavily on adopting digital invoicing solutions to minimize delays in receivables. Automated systems ensure timely delivery of invoices and reminders, reducing receivable periods significantly.

- **Example:** A logistics company in the U.S. implemented a digital invoicing system integrated with its CRM. As a result, receivable delays dropped by 30%, freeing up working capital for reinvestment in fleet expansion.
- **Lesson for Businesses:** Transition to digital invoicing tools like QuickBooks or Zoho Books to automate the receivables process, improve cash flow predictability, and enhance customer experience.

2. *Japanese Firms: Just-in-Time Inventory Systems*

- **Practice:** Japanese companies excel in cash flow management by adopting Just-in-Time (JIT) inventory systems. This approach minimizes holding costs by synchronizing inventory purchases with production schedules and demand forecasts.
- **Example:** A Japanese electronics manufacturer uses JIT to ensure components arrive just in time for assembly. This reduces excess inventory, freeing up cash for other operational needs.
- **Lesson for Businesses:** Explore JIT principles or inventory management tools to optimize stock levels and reduce cash tied up in unused inventory.

3. *European Focus on Long-Term Cash Flow Stability*

- **Practice:** European businesses prioritize building cash reserves and diversifying income streams to ensure long-term financial stability. They also leverage government subsidies and financial programs to maintain liquidity during economic fluctuations.

- **Example:** A German SME created a contingency fund by allocating 10% of monthly revenue to a reserve account. This strategy helped the business navigate cash flow challenges during an industry downturn without resorting to high-interest loans.
- **Lesson for Businesses:** Prioritize reserve building and long-term planning to weather economic uncertainties effectively.

4. Indian Businesses: Leveraging Technology for Cost Efficiency

- **Practice:** Indian businesses, especially SMEs, increasingly adopt affordable cloud-based solutions like Zoho Books to streamline cash flow management while keeping operational costs low.
- **Example:** A textile exporter in Surat switched to Zoho Books for invoicing and forecasting, reducing receivable periods and freeing up ₹50 lakhs in working capital.
- **Lesson for Businesses:** Invest in scalable, cost-effective technology to address cash flow challenges without burdening operational budgets.

5. Chinese Manufacturers: Supplier and Vendor Negotiations

- **Practice:** Chinese manufacturers emphasize negotiating favorable terms with suppliers, such as extended payment cycles or bulk discounts, to improve cash flow.
- **Example:** A Chinese toy manufacturer negotiated 90-day payment terms with suppliers while offering early-payment discounts to clients. This approach balanced cash inflows and outflows, enabling steady growth.

- **Lesson for Businesses:** Strengthen relationships with suppliers and negotiate terms that align with your cash flow needs.

Key Takeaways for Businesses

1. **Embrace Automation:**
   Whether through QuickBooks, Zoho Books, or SAP, leveraging automation tools improves accuracy and reduces delays in cash flow processes.
2. **Learn from JIT Systems:**
   Adopt inventory management practices that minimize holding costs and free up cash for other needs.
3. **Build Reserves:**
   Allocate a portion of your revenue to an emergency fund to manage unexpected disruptions.
4. **Global Inspiration, Local Application:**
   Adapt global practices to your local business environment. For instance, combine JIT principles with affordable tools like Microsoft Excel for inventory management.
5. **Focus on Forecasting:**
   Use advanced tools to predict cash flow needs and plan for seasonal or economic fluctuations.

By integrating these global practices and tools, businesses can transform their cash flow management and achieve sustainable growth, no matter their size or industry.

❍❍❍❍

CHAPTER 15

Practical Tools and Techniques for Cash Flow Management

Effective cash flow management is essential for business sustainability and growth. By utilizing practical tools and proven techniques, businesses can monitor, analyze, and optimize their cash flow. Below is a detailed guide on tools and methods to streamline cash flow management.

1. Cash Flow Statements: Manual Tracking Templates

What They Are:

A cash flow statement tracks the inflow and outflow of cash in a business, providing a clear picture of liquidity. It is essential for understanding operational, investing, and financing activities.

How to Use:

- Use templates in **Microsoft Excel** or **Google Sheets** to manually track cash movements.
- Break down cash flow into categories:
  - **Operating Activities:** Sales revenue, salaries, rent, etc.
  - **Investing Activities:** Equipment purchases, investments, etc.

- **Financing Activities:** Loan repayments, dividend payments, etc.

Practical Tools:

- **Templates:**
  - **Microsoft Excel:** Prebuilt cash flow statement templates with formulas.
  - **Google Sheets:** Free customizable templates for cloud-based access.
- **Apps:**
  - **Wave Accounting:** Free for small businesses to create simple cash flow reports.

Best Practice:

- Update the statement weekly or monthly to identify trends and anticipate shortfalls.

2. Budgeting Software: Recommendations for SMEs

What It Does:

Budgeting software helps businesses allocate resources efficiently, plan for expenses, and ensure that cash flow aligns with financial goals.

Recommended Tools:

1. **Zoho Books:**
   - Automated expense tracking and budgeting.
   - Visual dashboards for quick insights.
   - Integration with bank accounts for real-time updates.
   - Ideal for SMEs due to affordability and scalability.

2. **QuickBooks Online:**
   - Allows setting budgets based on historical data.
   - Tracks budget variances to identify overspending.
   - User-friendly interface and robust reporting capabilities.
3. **Xero:**
   - Cloud-based software for budgeting and cash flow forecasting.
   - Integration with payment gateways to streamline receivables.
4. **Microsoft Excel (Advanced Templates):**
   - Customizable templates for tailored budgeting needs.
   - Advanced formulas for detailed analysis, including cash flow projections.

Best Practice:

Use budgeting software to compare actual cash flow with planned budgets and adjust expenses or receivables as needed.

3. Ratio Analysis: Measuring Liquidity and Efficiency

What It Does:

Ratio analysis provides insights into the financial health of a business, helping you assess liquidity, operational efficiency, and solvency.

Key Ratios for Cash Flow Management:

1. **Current Ratio:**
   - Formula: Current Assets / Current Liabilities
   - Indicates whether the business can cover short-term liabilities with short-term assets.
   - Ideal Ratio: 1.5 to 2.

2. **Quick Ratio (Acid-Test Ratio):**
   - Formula: (Current Assets - Inventory) / Current Liabilities
   - Measures liquidity without relying on inventory, offering a stricter assessment.
   - Ideal Ratio: 1 to 1.5.
3. **Operating Cash Flow Ratio:**
   - Formula: Operating Cash Flow / Current Liabilities
   - Indicates whether a business generates enough cash to cover current obligations.
4. **Accounts Receivable Turnover Ratio:**
   - Formula: Net Credit Sales / Average Accounts Receivable
   - Tracks how efficiently the business collects payments.

Practical Tools:

- **Tally ERP:** Automates ratio calculations for liquidity and efficiency analysis.
- **Zoho Analytics:** Provides real-time dashboards for ratio tracking.

Best Practice:

Regularly analyze these ratios (monthly or quarterly) to make informed decisions about working capital and liquidity management.

4. Financial Forecasting Tools: Monthly and Quarterly Planning

---

What They Do:

Financial forecasting tools help predict cash flow needs based on historical trends, seasonal variations, and planned activities.

Recommended Tools:

1. **Float:**
    - Provides real-time cash flow forecasting.
    - Syncs with accounting tools like QuickBooks and Xero.
    - Offers scenario planning to test the impact of financial decisions.
2. **PlanGuru:**
    - Ideal for creating multi-year financial forecasts.
    - Integrates with accounting software for seamless data flow.
    - Allows tracking against KPIs to ensure accuracy.
3. **Microsoft Excel:**
    - Monthly and quarterly templates are available for free.
    - Use formulas like SUMIF, VLOOKUP, and pivot tables for detailed projections.
4. **How to Use Forecasting Tools:**
    - Create short-term (monthly) and long-term (quarterly/ annual) forecasts.
    - Include variables like seasonal sales trends, payment delays, and anticipated expenses.
    - Perform scenario analysis to plan for best-case, worst-case, and realistic outcomes.

Practical Templates:

- ➢ **Monthly Forecast Template:** Tracks inflows and outflows on a granular level.
- ➢ **Quarterly Forecast Template:** Provides a broader view of financial health, incorporating growth and investment plans.

5. Other Advanced Techniques for Cash Flow Management

A. Cash Flow Automation Tools

- Tools like Bill.com and Tipalti automate payment processing and streamline accounts payable and receivable management.
- They reduce manual errors and improve efficiency in managing multiple cash flow streams.

B. Cash Reserves Planning

- Allocate 10% of monthly revenue to an emergency fund.
- Use separate accounts to ensure reserves are not accidentally used.

C. Payment Term Adjustments

- Negotiate longer payment terms with suppliers (e.g., 60-90 days).
- Offer early payment discounts to clients to accelerate receivables.

Key Takeaways for Effective Cash Flow Management

1. **Adopt Digital Tools:** Leverage software like Zoho Books, QuickBooks, and Float to automate and simplify cash flow tracking.
2. **Monitor Ratios Regularly:** Analyze liquidity and efficiency using key financial ratios.

3. **Forecast Accurately:** Use templates or software to anticipate cash flow needs and prepare for fluctuations.
4. **Budget with Discipline:** Stick to well-planned budgets and adjust them as needed.
5. **Maintain Cash Reserves:** Build a safety net to manage unforeseen expenses or slow seasons.

By integrating these tools and techniques, businesses can gain control over their finances, minimize risks, and unlock new opportunities for growth.

❍❍❍❍

CHAPTER 16

Inspirational Stories from the Business World

The business world is filled with stories of visionaries who started with humble beginnings, faced immense challenges, and overcame them to create empires. These stories inspire us to dream big, persevere, and innovate despite the odds. Here, we explore the journeys of three remarkable individuals—Dhirubhai Ambani, Narayana Murthy, and Kiran Mazumdar-Shaw—who turned their aspirations into global success stories.

1. Dhirubhai Ambani:
From Petrol Pump Attendant to Building Reliance

The Journey:

Born in Chorwad, a small village in Gujarat, **Dhirubhai Ambani** started his career as a petrol pump attendant in Yemen. His modest beginnings taught him the value of hard work, perseverance, and ambition. Despite limited resources, he dreamt of building a business empire in India.

The Challenges:

- Lack of financial backing and formal education.
- Navigating a highly regulated Indian economy in the 1960s and 70s.

- Competing against established players with deep-rooted connections.

The Breakthrough:

Dhirubhai returned to India and started Reliance Commercial Corporation in 1958, trading in spices, yarn, and other commodities. His strategic insights into India's growing need for synthetic fabrics led him to set up a textile manufacturing unit.

Innovative Approach:

- **Public Trust:** Dhirubhai democratized investment by launching India's first Initial Public Offering (IPO) in 1977, inviting ordinary citizens to invest in Reliance.
- **Vertical Integration:** He ensured complete control of the supply chain by expanding Reliance into petrochemicals, refining, and polyester production.
- **Visionary Leadership:** He focused on long-term growth, always reinvesting profits into expanding the business.

The Legacy:

Dhirubhai's relentless drive transformed Reliance Industries into one of India's largest conglomerates, spanning energy, textiles, telecommunications, and retail. His journey proves that a bold vision, combined with determination and innovation, can overcome any obstacle.

2. Narayana Murthy: Leveraging Small Capital to Create Infosys

The Journey:

In 1981, Narayana Murthy co-founded Infosys with an initial capital of ₹10,000 borrowed from his wife, Sudha Murthy. The company began as a small software export firm with seven employees and grew into one of the world's leading IT services companies.

The Challenges:

- Operating in a pre-liberalized Indian economy with strict regulations.
- Limited access to international markets and technological infrastructure.
- Convincing global clients to trust an Indian IT company.

The Breakthrough:

Murthy's ability to foresee the global shift toward information technology helped Infosys carve a niche in the global market. He emphasized delivering value to clients through innovation and quality service.

Innovative Approach:

- **Client Focus:** He instilled a culture of prioritizing client satisfaction by delivering high-quality solutions on time.
- **Employee Empowerment:** Infosys became one of the first Indian companies to introduce stock options for employees, aligning their success with the company's growth.
- **Transparency:** Infosys set new benchmarks for corporate governance and financial disclosure, earning global credibility.

The Legacy:

Today, Infosys is a global leader in IT services, employing over 300,000 people and generating billions in revenue annually. Murthy's story shows how disciplined execution, ethical leadership, and a global vision can turn a small idea into a global powerhouse.

3. Kiran Mazumdar-Shaw: Managing Cash Flow Hurdles to Establish Biocon

The Journey:

Kiran Mazumdar-Shaw started Biocon in 1978 in a small garage in Bengaluru with just ₹10,000 as seed capital. Her initial aim was to produce industrial enzymes, but her vision soon expanded to include biopharmaceuticals.

The Challenges:

- Gender bias in securing funding and partnerships.
- Severe cash flow issues in the initial stages, with many lenders refusing to back her due to her lack of a business background.
- Limited infrastructure and expertise in biotechnology in India at the time.

The Breakthrough:

Despite financial constraints, Kiran leveraged her technical expertise as a trained brewer and her determination to innovate. She built Biocon brick by brick, convincing investors and partners of the potential of biotechnology.

Innovative Approach:

- **Strategic Partnerships:** Kiran partnered with foreign companies to gain access to technology and markets.
- **Managing Cash Flow:** To overcome funding challenges, she focused on generating revenue through industrial enzyme sales while gradually expanding into biopharmaceuticals.

- **R&D Investment:** She invested heavily in research and development to ensure Biocon stayed ahead of competitors.

The Legacy:

Under Kiran's leadership, Biocon became India's leading biotechnology company, producing affordable life-saving drugs and pioneering research in diabetes, oncology, and immunology. Her resilience and resourcefulness demonstrate how to turn financial challenges into stepping stones for success.

Lessons from These Inspirational Stories

1. **Dream Big, Start Small:** Dhirubhai Ambani and Narayana Murthy began with humble resources but had grand visions that drove their determination to succeed.
2. **Overcome Challenges with Innovation:** Kiran Mazumdar-Shaw showed how to navigate financial hurdles through strategic planning and partnerships.
3. **Value People:** Narayana Murthy's emphasis on transparency and employee empowerment created a strong foundation for Infosys.
4. **Adapt to Changing Times:** Dhirubhai Ambani's ability to foresee market trends helped Reliance diversify and dominate multiple industries.
5. **Persevere Through Adversity:** All three leaders faced immense challenges but remained steadfast in their commitment to their goals.

Inspiration for Aspiring Entrepreneurs

These stories inspire us to believe that no matter how modest our beginnings or how daunting the challenges, success is achievable with:

- **Visionary Thinking:** Seeing opportunities where others see obstacles.
- **Resilience:** Staying committed to your goals despite setbacks.
- **Adaptability:** Evolving with market demands and technological advancements.
- **Innovation:** Continuously improving and finding creative solutions.

If Dhirubhai Ambani, Narayana Murthy, and Kiran Mazumdar-Shaw could transform their industries, you too can turn your dreams into reality with courage, persistence, and the right strategies. Let their journeys motivate you to embark on your own path to greatness.

❍❍❍❍

CHAPTER 17

Financial Contingency Planning

Financial contingency planning is the process of preparing your business to handle unexpected disruptions, economic downturns, or emergencies. A well-structured contingency plan ensures that your business remains resilient, even in the face of unforeseen challenges like market volatility, supply chain disruptions, or cash flow shortages.

Below is a detailed and actionable framework for creating a robust financial contingency plan.

1. Create a 10% Reserve Fund from Monthly Revenues

Why It's Important:

A reserve fund acts as a financial cushion to manage unexpected expenses, revenue shortfalls, or emergencies. This fund provides liquidity when cash inflows slow down or operational costs increase suddenly.

How to Implement:

1. **Set a Fixed Percentage:**
    - Dedicate 10% of your monthly revenue to a contingency fund. This ensures consistent contributions regardless of business performance.

2. **Separate the Reserve:**
    - Open a dedicated account for the reserve fund to prevent its accidental use.
    - Use high-interest savings accounts or liquid mutual funds to earn returns while maintaining accessibility.
3. **Automate Savings:**
    - Automate fund transfers from your operating account to the reserve account to ensure discipline.
4. **Define Rules for Use:**
    - Clearly outline situations where the fund can be used, such as covering payroll during a revenue dip or addressing urgent equipment repairs.

Benefits:

- ➢ Provides immediate liquidity during crises.
- ➢ Reduces dependency on borrowing.
- ➢ Builds confidence among stakeholders like employees, suppliers, and investors.

2. Prepare for Market Downturns with Predictive Modeling

Why It's Important:

Market downturns, economic slowdowns, or sector-specific challenges can impact revenue streams and cash flow. Predictive modeling helps businesses anticipate and prepare for such scenarios.

How to Implement:

1. **Use Historical Data:**
    - Analyze past financial data to identify patterns during previous downturns.
    - Assess how factors like seasonal demand, geopolitical events, or industry-specific trends impacted your business.
2. **Leverage Predictive Tools:**
    - Tools like PlanGuru, Float, or QuickBooks Advanced Forecasting can model financial scenarios.
    - Use these tools to forecast revenue, expenses, and cash flow for multiple scenarios:
3. **Best-case scenario: Moderate growth.**
    - Worst-case scenario: Significant revenue drop.
    - Realistic scenario: Average market performance.
4. **Monitor Key Indicators:**
    - Track leading economic indicators like inflation rates, interest rates, and consumer spending.
    - Stay updated on industry reports to spot early warning signs of downturns.
5. **Adjust Operational Plans:**
    - Prepare cost-cutting measures such as reducing discretionary spending, delaying expansion plans, or renegotiating vendor contracts.
    - Plan for workforce adjustments, such as cross-training employees to manage critical functions.

Benefits:

- Minimizes the impact of market volatility.
- Allows proactive decision-making.
- Helps maintain stability during uncertain periods.

3. Establish Emergency Credit Lines with Banks

Why It's Important:

An emergency credit line provides immediate access to funds during financial crises. Unlike loans, credit lines offer flexibility, allowing businesses to borrow only what they need and repay as cash flow stabilizes.

How to Implement:

1. **Research and Choose the Right Credit Line:**
    - Compare products like overdraft facilities, revolving credit lines, and business credit cards.
    - Evaluate interest rates, fees, and repayment terms.
2. **Build Strong Banking Relationships:**
    - Maintain a healthy relationship with your bank by ensuring regular communication and transparency.
    - Share your financial health reports to demonstrate creditworthiness.
3. **Negotiate Favorable Terms:**
    - Request competitive interest rates and higher credit limits based on your business performance and collateral.
    - Explore government-backed credit schemes for SMEs, which often come with lower interest rates.

4. **Maintain Eligibility:**
   - Keep your financial records updated and accurate.
   - Ensure your credit score is strong by paying existing debts on time and avoiding defaults.
5. **Use Wisely:**
   - Reserve the credit line for emergencies only, such as covering payroll during revenue gaps or fulfilling critical supplier payments to avoid disruptions.

Benefits:

- Provides instant access to funds during crises.
- Reduces the need for high-interest emergency loans.
- Offers financial flexibility to manage short-term cash shortages.

Other Key Components of Financial Contingency Planning

A. Diversify Income Streams:

- Reduce reliance on a single product, client, or market.
- Introduce complementary services or target new customer segments to stabilize revenue.

B. Secure Business Insurance:

- Invest in insurance policies for critical risks such as property damage, liability claims, or business interruptions.
- Evaluate specialized coverage options like cyber insurance or supply chain insurance based on your industry.

C. Review and Update Regularly:

- Conduct quarterly reviews of your contingency plan to adapt to changing market conditions or internal business dynamics.
- Incorporate feedback from key stakeholders, such as employees, partners, and investors.

Real-Life Examples of Financial Contingency Planning

Example 1: A Retail Business Building Reserves

- A small retail business in Jaipur consistently allocated 10% of its monthly revenue to a reserve fund. When the COVID-19 lockdown disrupted operations, the business used its reserves to cover rent and salaries for three months. This financial preparedness allowed the store to reopen seamlessly post-lockdown.

Example 2: Manufacturing Firm Preparing for Downturns

- A manufacturing firm in Pune used predictive modeling to prepare for raw material shortages during a global supply chain crisis. By forecasting the impact of price hikes, the firm secured long-term supplier contracts at fixed rates, saving ₹50 lakhs over a year.

Example 3: SME Leveraging Emergency Credit

- An SME in Bengaluru established an overdraft facility of ₹25 lakhs with its bank. When a key client delayed payments by two months, the company used the overdraft to pay suppliers on time, avoiding production delays and maintaining client trust.

Benefits of Financial Contingency Planning

1. **Business Continuity:** Ensures uninterrupted operations during crises.
2. **Stakeholder Confidence:** Builds trust among employees, suppliers, and investors.
3. **Reduced Stress:** Prepares the business for emergencies, minimizing panic-driven decisions.
4. **Sustainable Growth:** Allows businesses to navigate challenges without derailing long-term plans.

Call to Action: Start Planning Today

Financial contingency planning is not a luxury; it's a necessity in today's unpredictable business environment. Whether you're a small business owner or a large enterprise, implementing these strategies can safeguard your financial future.

Start today by:

- Creating a reserve fund.
- Using predictive modeling for market insights.
- Establishing emergency credit lines.

Prepare now to protect your business and seize opportunities, even in the face of uncertainty.

CHAPTER 18

FAQs and Glossary

Cash Flow Management FAQs

Here are 21 frequently asked questions (FAQs) about cash flow management, along with detailed answers and a glossary of essential terms to help you understand the key concepts.

FAQs

1. **What is cash flow forecasting?**

   Answer: Cash flow forecasting is the process of predicting the inflows (receivables) and outflows (expenses) of cash over a specific period. It helps businesses anticipate cash shortages or surpluses and plan accordingly. **Example:** A retail business might forecast cash flow for the holiday season to ensure adequate inventory and staffing. **Tools:** Excel templates, QuickBooks, and Float.

2. **How do I manage receivables effectively?**

   Answer: Managing receivables involves ensuring customers pay on time. Best practices include:

   - Automating invoicing and sending reminders.
   - Offering discounts for early payments.
   - Enforcing penalties for late payments.

   Example: A textile exporter reduced receivables from 90 days to 45 days by automating reminders.

3. **Why is cash flow different from profit?**

   Answer: Profit is the financial gain after expenses, while cash flow refers to actual cash movement. A business can be profitable but face cash flow issues if receivables are delayed or inventory is overstocked.

4. **What are the main types of cash flows?**

   Answer:

   - **Operating Cash Flow:** Day-to-day business operations.
   - **Investing Cash Flow:** Purchases or sales of assets.
   - **Financing Cash Flow:** Loans, dividends, and equity-related activities.

5. **How do I prepare a cash flow statement?**

   Answer:

   - List all cash inflows and outflows.
   - Categorize them into operating, investing, and financing activities.
   - Calculate the net cash flow.
   - **Tools:** Microsoft Excel, Tally ERP.

6. **How can I reduce cash flow shortages?**

   Answer:

   - Build a reserve fund.
   - Negotiate better payment terms with vendors.
   - Optimize inventory levels to free up cash.

7. **What is the importance of working capital in cash flow?**

   Answer: Working capital is the difference between current assets and liabilities. Positive working capital ensures you have enough cash to cover short-term expenses.

8. **How does inventory affect cash flow?**

   Answer: Excess inventory ties up cash, while insufficient inventory can lead to lost sales. Implement tools like Just-in-Time (JIT) to optimize inventory levels.

9. **How do I prepare for seasonal cash flow fluctuations?**

   Answer:

   - Use historical data to forecast revenue and expenses.
   - Build a reserve fund during peak seasons.
   - Negotiate flexible repayment terms with suppliers.

10. **What is a cash flow reserve fund?**

    Answer: A cash flow reserve fund is a dedicated account where a percentage of revenue (e.g., 10%) is saved to handle emergencies or slow periods.

11. **What are cash flow KPIs?**

    Answer: Key Performance Indicators (KPIs) for cash flow include:

    - Current Ratio
    - Quick Ratio
    - Operating Cash Flow Ratio
    - Accounts Receivable Turnover

12. **How do I automate cash flow management?**

    Answer: Use tools like QuickBooks, Zoho Books, or SAP to automate invoicing, track expenses, and generate cash flow reports.

13. **What is the difference between direct and indirect cash flow methods?**

    Answer:

    - **Direct Method:** Tracks actual cash transactions.

- **Indirect Method:** Adjusts net income for non-cash items to calculate cash flow.

14. How do I handle late payments from clients?

Answer:

- Establish clear payment terms in contracts.
- Use automated reminders.
- Enforce penalties for late payments or offer discounts for early payments.

15. What is the role of financial forecasting in cash flow management?

Answer: Forecasting helps predict future cash needs, allowing businesses to plan for expenses, secure funding, and avoid shortages.

16. How do I manage cash flow during a crisis?

Answer:

- Use emergency credit lines.
- Prioritize essential expenses.
- Reevaluate payment terms with vendors and clients.

17. What are the risks of poor cash flow management?

Answer:

- Inability to pay suppliers or employees.
- Missed growth opportunities.

➢ Increased reliance on high-interest loans.

18. Can cash flow management improve profitability?

Answer: Yes. Efficient cash flow management reduces financing costs, improves operational efficiency, and allows reinvestment in growth areas.

19. How do I integrate cash flow management with other business functions?

Answer: Align cash flow strategies with sales, procurement, and marketing to ensure all departments contribute to financial stability.

20. How do I track cash flow manually?

Answer: Use Excel templates or Google Sheets to log daily inflows and outflows. Categorize them and update balances regularly.

21. What is the best tool for small businesses to manage cash flow?

Answer: For small businesses, Zoho Books and QuickBooks are affordable, user-friendly tools with automation features.

❍❍❍❍

Glossary of Key Terms

1. **Net Cash Flow:**

   The difference between total cash inflows and outflows during a specific period. Positive net cash flow indicates liquidity, while negative indicates a shortfall.

2. **Working Capital:**

   The difference between current assets and current liabilities. It reflects a company's ability to cover short-term obligations.

3. **Operating Cash Flow (OCF):**

   Cash generated from core business operations, excluding investments and financing.

4. **Quick Ratio:**

   A liquidity ratio measuring a company's ability to pay short-term obligations without relying on inventory. Formula: (Current Assets - Inventory) / Current Liabilities

5. **Current Ratio:**

   A liquidity ratio that measures a company's ability to pay short-term liabilities with short-term assets. Formula: Current Assets / Current Liabilities

6. **Accounts Receivable Turnover:**

   A measure of how efficiently a company collects receivables. Formula: Net Credit Sales / Average Accounts Receivable

7. **Just-in-Time (JIT):**

   An inventory management system where stock is purchased or produced only when needed, minimizing holding costs.

8. **Cash Flow Reserve Fund:**

   A dedicated savings account used to manage emergencies or slow revenue periods.

9. **Direct Cash Flow Method:**

   Tracks actual cash transactions, providing a straightforward view of cash movements.

10. **Indirect Cash Flow Method:**

    Starts with net income and adjusts for non-cash transactions and changes in working capital to calculate cash flow.

CHAPTER 19

To Conclude It All

Cash flow mastery is not a destination but a journey. With the strategies and examples provided, you can transform your business into a financially secure and thriving enterprise. Let's embark on this journey to financial freedom together.

As a reader of this book, you have proven that you are serious about ending your cash flow struggles and running your business smoothly.

As a reward for being an action-taker, I have a FREE Gift for you—-

Get Access to my life & business-changing webinar

CASH FLOW MASTERY

Instantly end Cash arranging struggle and enjoy peace of mind, freedom, and more profits without making complex financial calculations or analysis

Feel the weight of financial stress lifting off your shoulders as overdue payments disappear. Enjoy the ease of running a business that's cash flow-positive

End cash worries and enjoy more profits, freedom, and peace of mind with easy strategies

Here are the phenomenal results you can expect from this webinar

- Timely Collections
- Debt-Free Growth
- Robust Cash Reserves
- Sustainable Passive Income
- Vendor Satisfaction
- Efficient Accounting System
- Simplified Payment Processes

SCAN THE QR CODE BELOW TO BOOK YOUR SPOT

OOOO

www.ingramcontent.com/pod-product-compliance
Ingram Content Group UK Ltd.
Pitfield, Milton Keynes, MK11 3LW, UK
UKHW021656190726
13853UKWH00001B/293

9 789363 389960